THE BOOK OF
SLIME

A KID'S GUIDE ON HOW TO MAKE THE **BEST SLIMES** OF ALL TIME

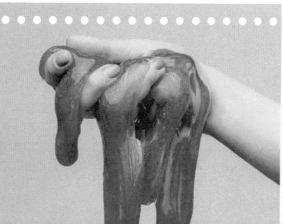

Warnings for Slime
PARENTAL SUPERVISION ALWAYS REQUIRED*
Slime is not edible. DO NOT EAT. If ingested, seek medical help immediately.
Wash your hands before and after playing with slime
Not suitable for ages below 4
CHOKING HAZARD - MAY CONTAIN SMALL PARTS
All of our recipes contain Borax ☠. Do not let children handle borax powder or mixture. ALWAYS have an adult mix in the borax mixture or "activator". Use gloves if you feel it is necessary. Borax can result in skin irritation when exposure is repeated or prolonged. Read all Borax labels and follow packages instructions.
Peanut Prodigy is not responsible for any accidents that may occur.

SLIIIIIIIIIME!

It's ooey, it's gooey, and it's **SO FUN** to play with! Slime is our newest obsession. There are so many different variations, and the number of combos you can create are endless. Different beads, glitter, colors...talk about hours and hours of fun! Making slime is perfect for sleepovers or curing those Saturday afternoon boredom blues. We've put together the Book of Slime just for you! Whether you're a newbie or an expert, you can use our recipes to create the ultimate slime over and over again!

THINGS YOU WILL NEED

Sometimes it's hard to find everything you need to make slime. Luckily for you, we've created a list of items you will need for the recipes in this book - some you will have on hand, and some you may need to stock up on.

1. Elmer's School Glue
You will need both clear and white glue for the recipes found in this book. Making slime is a fun and addictive hobby, so we buy the gallon-size glue containers (found on Amazon). If you're just looking to make one or two slime recipes, the smaller sized glue found at any craft store will work great!

2. Borax
An odd ingredient that's not always easy to find. You can typically find it at Walmart.

3. Shaving Cream
Found at any grocery store or dollar store!

4. Contact Solution
Must contain sodium borate (ask your parents about this one).

5. Foaming Hand Soap
Any kind works!

6. Foaming Face Wash

7. Lotion

8. Big Bowls

9. Rubber Spatula

With slime, the options are truly endless. All it takes to make the greatest slime of all time is some creativity and time! Take a trip to the dollar store and find some beads, glitters, paints, anything fun that you would like to add in your slime!

In this book, we will show you some of our favorite slimes, but after that...it's all up to your imagination! Colors and textures can be changed in every slime recipe, so if you have an idea, try it! Using the basic fluffy slime and basic clear slime is a great place to start. Add in whatever color and extra features you want!

HERE ARE SOME OF OUR FAVORITE ADD INS:

Clay
Daiso clay or Model Magic is a key ingredient to making butter slimes and soft clay-like slimes! Daiso can be found on Amazon in a variety of colors, or you can stop by any local craft store and pick up Model Magic Clay.

Glitter
This can really amp up a slime recipe, especially if you use different colors and sizes of glitter!

Fake Snow
Easily found on Amazon.

Plastic Filler Beads
This is how you make crunchy slime, can be found on Amazon or in a craft store.

Beads
Can be any kind of beads! Get creative and stop by the dollar store or Amazon.

Magnetic Powder
Found at Walmart or online.

Sprinkles
Colorful additions as well as great for texture in slimes.

Water Based Paint
This is great for pigmentation in your slimes. Doesn't need to be anything fancy, you can pick some up at the dollar store or any craft store!

Foam Beads
This is how we make our FLOAM Slime, can be found online or at a craft store.

Glow Powder
Can be found online, search glow in the dark powder.

LET'S GET THE FUN STARTED!

ACTIVATOR

You'll need an activator in every single recipe in this book. The activator is what takes your glue mixture and makes it a SLIME. Feel free to double this recipe so you'll always have some on hand.

Ingredients:

★ 1 teaspoon Borax Powder
★ 1 cup Hot Water

Directions:

1) In a bowl, add in 1 teaspoon of borax and 1 cup hot water and stir until dissolved.

2) Pour mixture into a bottle and keep on hand for slime recipes. You will need this ingredient for most recipes.

BASIC FLUFFY SLIME

Fluffy slime is exactly what it sounds like, pure fluff! We've perfected this recipe for you, so it's a great starting point for all slimes. Once you get this recipe down, use your imagination for color combinations and test your abilities to make the greatest slime of all time!

Ingredients:

- ★ 1 cup white glue
- ★ 1/2 cup water
- ★ 4 cups shaving cream
- ★ 2 tablespoon contact solu
- ★ 2-3 tablespoons of activator

Directions:

1) Combine glue, water, and shaving cream to a large bowl.

2) Fold in contact solution.

3) Add in your activator one tablespoon at a time until combined.

4) Knead until smooth and soft!

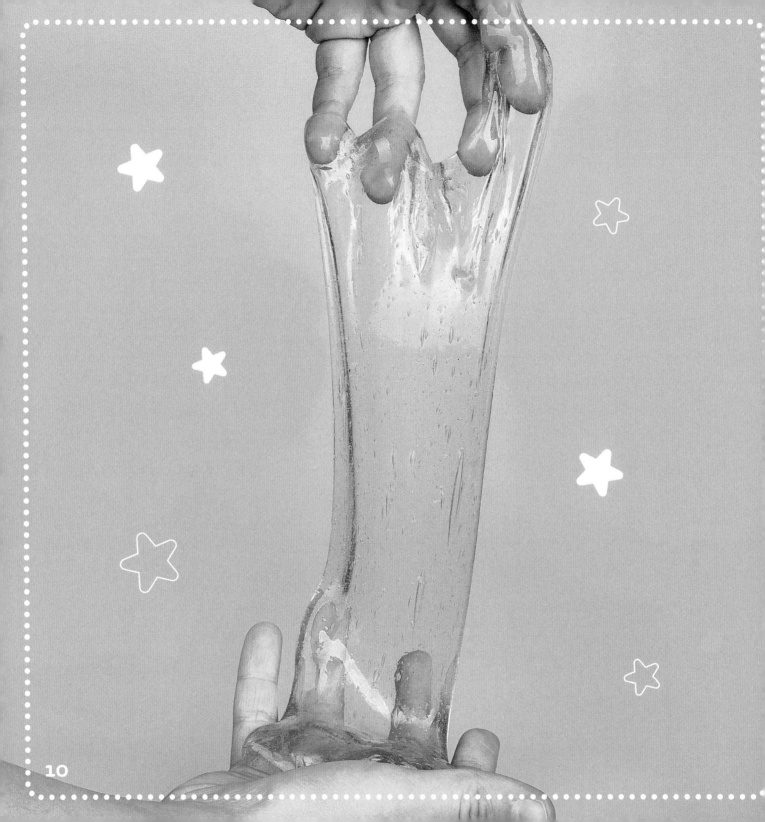

★ BASIC GOOEY SLIME ★

Gooey slime is cold, shiny, and so much FUN. Use this recipe as the base of all your shiny gooey slime creations!

Ingredients:

★ 1 1/2 cup Clear glue
★ Activator

Directions:

1) Add the clear glue to a bowl, and slowly activate your glue.

2) Clear glue activates quicker than white, so start with a half a tablespoon of activator and add more if needed.

3) Knead until smooth and not too sticky!

11

GIANT PINK MARSHMALLOW SLIME

Directions:

1) Combine the school glue and water in a large bowl and stir very well making a liquid-y consistency.

2) Add in your food coloring, more or less depending on how pink you want your slime! You can also use any color you'd like.

3) Add in your shaving cream, about 1 cup at a time, stirring in between. Stir until combined fully.

4) Add in your two pinches of baking soda and combine.

5) Squirt in your lens solution, a little at a time until you find a slime texture you like! You do not have to use the whole ¼ cup.

6) Take your slime out of the bowl and knead it until fully smooth!

Ingredients:

★ 1 1/2 cup of white school glue
★ ¼ cup of water
★ Food coloring
★ 3 cups of shaving cream
★ 2 pinches of baking soda
★ 1/4 cup of lens solution
★ Bowl
★ Rubber Spatula

13

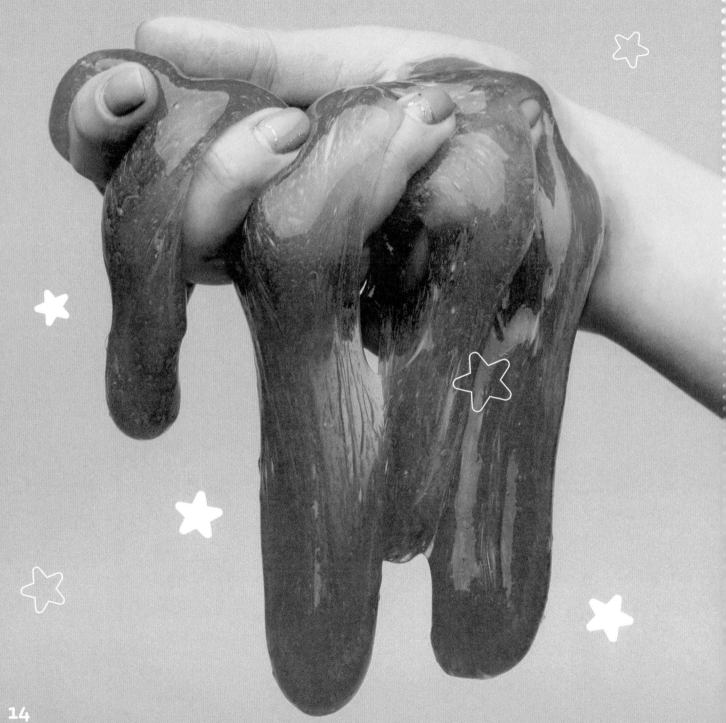

IRIDESCENT BARBIE SLIME

Directions:

1) Combine the glue and the water in a large bowl.

2) Add in your gold fine glitter, and mix well. Then add in your pink coloring.

3) Stir in your baking soda.

4) Lastly, add in your saline solution and mix until the slime is coming off the edges of the bowl.

5) We suggest you knead your slime for a few minutes to improve consistency and texture!

Ingredients:

- 1/2 cup Clear or White PVA School Glue
- 1 tablespoon Saline Solution (must contain boric acid and sodium borate)
- 1/2 cup of Water
- 1/4-1/2 teaspoon Baking Soda
- Pink coloring
- Gold fine glitter

 # BUTTER SLIME

Directions:

1) Measure 3-4 heaping cups of shaving cream into a bowl. You can also experiment with using less shaving cream for different textures!

2) Add color! We used neon food coloring, but there are so many choices!

3) Next, add a 1/2 cup of glue to the shaving cream and mix.

4) Add 1/2 teaspoon of baking soda and mix.

5) Add 1 tablespoon of the contact solution to the mixture and start whipping! Once your done whipping the slime together, you can pull it out of your bowl and start kneading it.

6) Once your fluffy slime is incorporated together, add your clump of clay. This is what makes your clay "buttery" soft! It may be hard to incorporate, or make your slime too dry. If this is the case, add some moisturizer to your slime.

7) Enjoy!

Ingredients:

★ 3-4 Cups Shaving Cream
★ Yellow Food Coloring
★ ½ cup White School Glue
★ ½ teaspoon Baking Soda
★ 1 tablespoon contact solution
★ Daiso Clay or Model Magic Clay (white)
★ Moisturizing lotion

UNICORN POOP SLIME

Directions:

1) Add your glue, water, and shaving cream into the large bowl.

2) Next, fold in contact solution.

3) Now, activate your slime! Add in one tablespoon of your activator at a time and mix until the consistency you want.

4) Begin kneading, if your slime is too sticky, add in a little more borax mixture.

5) Once your slime is complete, separate it into 3 to 4 pieces depending on your colors.

6) Knead in your colors into the slime.

7) Combine all pieces and gently twist them together until you're happy with your unicorn colors!

Ingredients:

★ 1 cup White Glue
★ ½ cup Water
★ 3-4 cups Shaving cream
★ 2 tablespoons contact solution
★ 3-4 tablespoons Activator
★ 3-4 different colors (Pink, Yellow, Blue, and Purple)
★ Large Bowl

19

 # FLOAM SLIME

Directions:

1) Start by combining your glue, coloring and glitter if you are adding them to your slime!

2) Then, activate your slime with 1 teaspoon of activator at a time. We want this slime to be a little stickier than normal, so the foam beads will stay in the slime and not pop out.

3) Once your slime is activated, pour the slime over your foam beads and knead them into the slime.

4) If your slime is too sticky, add some more beads!

5) Enjoy your homemade floam!

Ingredients:

- ★ 1 Cup Clear Glue
- ★ Coloring (Optional)
- ★ Iridescent Glitter (optional)
- ★ Activator
- ★ 1-2 cups Foam Beads

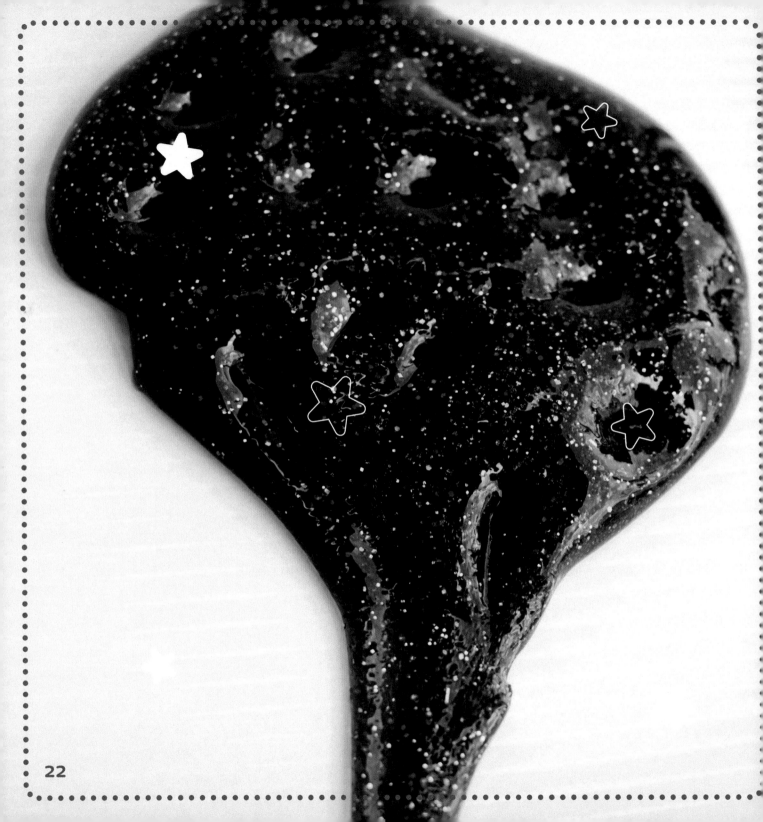

GALAXY SLIME

Directions:

1) Add your glue, colorings, and glitters to your bowl and mix well.

2) Slowly add in activator 1 teaspoon at a time until fully activated.

3) Knead together until your slime is smooth and not sticky!

4) Enjoy your galactic slime!

Ingredients:

★ 1 cup Clear Glue

★ Paint (a drop or two of black and blue)

★ Glitter (multiple colors and sizes, we use white and silver)

★ Activator

PINK CRUNCHY SLIME

Directions:

1) Add your glue, coloring, and glitter into a bowl and mix well.

2) Activate your glue with 1 teaspoon of activator at a time, until almost fully activated.

3) Pour your slime over your filler beads and knead in mixture until fully combined! If your slime is too sticky, add in more beads!

Ingredients:

- ★ 1 cup clear glue
- ★ Pink acrylic paint
- ★ Iridescent glitter (optional)
- ★ Activator
- ★ 1-2 cups Plastic Filler Beads

25

CLOUD SLIME

Directions:

1) Combine your glue and paint in a bowl and mix well!

2) Activate your glue 1 teaspoon at a time until fully activated.

3) In a separate bowl, follow package instructions for your instant snow. Once your snow is created, combine one cup of snow with your slime. Add more if needed!

4) Enjoy your cloud-like snow!

Ingredients:
- ★ 1 cup white glue
- ★ Purple paint
- ★ Activator
- ★ Instant snow

ITALIAN ICE SNOW

Directions:

1) Combine glue, cornstarch, shaving foam, and coloring into your bowl and mix well.

2) Activate your slime one tablespoon at a time, until fully activated.

3) Add in your instant snow and combine.

4) Mix in your clay for the final touch to your Italian Ice Snow Cone Slime!

Ingredients:

★ 1 cup White Glue
★ 1 tablespoon cornstarch
★ 1 cup Shaving foam
★ Food Coloring, we did blue for Blue Raspberry Italian Ice
★ Activator
★ Instant Snow
★ Clay

LEMON POPPY SEED FOAM SLIME

Directions:

1) Add your glue, soap, and food coloring, and glitter into your bowl and mix well.

2) Activate your glue 1 tablespoon at a time until fully activated.

3) Knead your slime until smooth and not sticky!

4) Enjoy your lemon poppyseed slime!

Ingredients:

- ★ 1 cup White glue
- ★ 8 pumps of any foaming hand soap
- ★ Yellow food coloring
- ★ Black Glitter
- ★ Activator

31

RAINBOW CHIP SLIME

Directions:

1) Combine your clear glue and white paint into your bowl and mix well.

2) Activate your slime, mixing in 1 teaspoon at a time until almost fully activated. Leave it a little sticky.

3) Pour slime over your multicolored foam beads to create Rainbow Chip Floam.

Ingredients:

★ 1 1/2 cup clear glue
★ White acrylic paint
★ Activator
★ Multicolor Foam Beads

★ MAGNETIC SLIME ★

Directions:

1) Add glue and water into a bowl and mix well.

2) Activate your slime, 1 teaspoon at a time.

3) Once fully activated, knead in your Black Iron Oxide Powder.

4) Once fully incorporated, you have magnetic slime! Test it out with your Neodymium Magnet.

Ingredients:

★ 1 cup white glue

★ ½ cup water

★ Activator

★ 2-4 teaspoons Black Iron Oxide Powder

★ Neodymium Magnet

35

ICEBERG SLIME

Directions:

1) Combine glue and shaving cream to a large bowl.

2) Fold in food coloring.

3) Add in your activator one tablespoon at a time until combined.

4) Knead until smooth and soft.

5) Now here's the hard part, leave your slime out, uncovered, for at least two days. This will allow it to dry out on the top, and create the "iceberg" layer.

6) After two days, play with your iceberg slime! We recommend taking full advantage of the new texture on top, so we like to poke holes in it and play with the top until the iceberg layer is gone!

Ingredients:

★ 1 cup white glue
★ 4 cups shaving cream
★ Blue Food Coloring
★ Activator

37

CHARCOAL SLIME

Directions:

1) Combine your glue, hand soap, face wash, shaving cream, and black paint in a large bowl.

2) Activate your slime and knead until smooth.

3) Fold in your clay until you have the soft texture of butter slime!

4) Enjoy!

Ingredients:

- 1 cup white glue
- 5 pumps foaming hand soap
- 3 pumps foaming face wash
- 2 cups shaving cream
- Black paint
- Activator
- Black Clay

 ★ # MERMAID SLIME ★

Directions:

1) Pour your glue into a bowl and fully activate.

2) Once activated, knead until smooth and no longer sticky.

3) Separate your slime into 3 pieces.

4) Add food coloring and glitter to each piece, then knead until fully incorporated.

5) Twist your pieces of slime together, and combine them!

6) Enjoy your slime from another dimension!

Ingredients:
- ★ 1 1/2 cup clear glue
- ★ Activator
- ★ Food Coloring (purple, blue, and pink)
- ★ Glitter (Silver iridescent)

41

GLOW IN THE DARK SLIME

Directions:

1) Add the clear glue and glow powder to a bowl and mix well.

2) Pour in the activator and slowly activate your glue until your slime forms.

3) Knead until smooth and not too sticky.

4) Test out your slime in the dark!

Ingredients:

★ 1 1/2 cup Clear glue

★ 1 Tablespoon Glow Powder

★ Activator

COLOR CHANGING SLIME

Directions:

1) Add glue, water, food coloring, and thermochromic powder to a bowl and mix well.

2) Activate your slime with 1 tablespoon of activator at a time.

3) Once fully combined, knead until smooth and no longer sticky.

Ingredients:

- 1 cup white glue
- ¼ cup water
- 1 tablespoon yellow thermochromic pigment
- Red Food coloring
- Activator

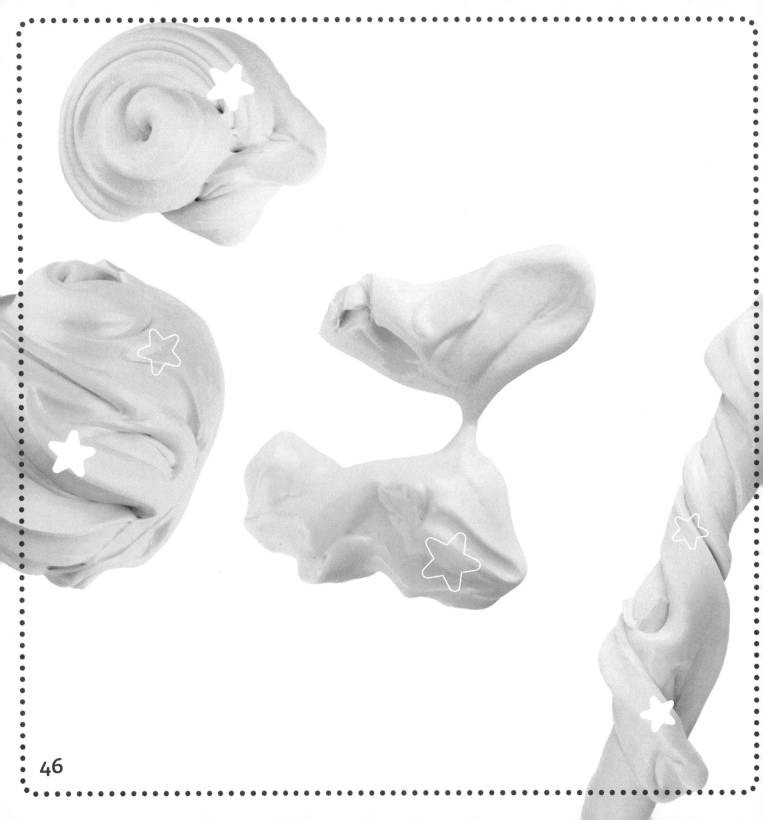

COTTON CANDY SLIME

Directions:

1) Combine glue, water, and shaving cream to a large bowl.

2) Fold in contact solution.

3) Add in your activator one tablespoon at a time until combined.

4) Knead until smooth and soft!

5) Separate your slime into two pieces, and add your colors to each piece.

6) Twist and combine your slime to make cotton candy slime!

Ingredients:

- ★ 1 cup white glue
- ★ 1/2 cup water
- ★ 4 cups shaving cream
- ★ 2 tbsp contact solution
- ★ 2-3 Tablespoons of Activator
- ★ Pink and Blue Food Coloring

THANKS SO MUCH FOR GOING THROUGH OUR BOOK!

I hope you and your friends and family have had a lot of sticky fun making our slime! Send us all your best and worst slime pictures to peanutprodigypublishing@gmail.com and we will pick a random winner for a $25 Amazon gift card!